PRAISE FOR THAT LITTLE GIRL

That Little Girl is full of touching moments of one girl's challenges to make sense of her life. We hear the voice of a child and teenager honoring the relationships that contributed to her spiritual formation.

Belva Brown Jordan
Former President of Disciples Seminary Foundation

That Little Girl is a beautiful collection of love letters that reminds us of the complex bonds shared by family members — young and old. Bravo, Dr. Charisse L. Gillett for this rich tapestry!

Angela Tuck
Author of "Somewhere Listening for my Name: 1960s Activists Tell Their Stories"

That Little Girl is a joy! I know first-hand the dreams and anxieties of being a "girl dad." It's a rewarding journey, but you don't see the outcome until decades later. This book is a moment to catch glimpses of that outcome and reflect on my journey as a parent.

Rev. B. Chris Dorsey
President Disciples Home Mission

To be known and loved by siblings and friends is a powerful way to enter and move through the world. Little girls come from somewhere, and Dr. Gillett has shared a small window of where she is from.

Carla R. Ross, CPA/MBA
Director of Finance, UIC Department of Psychiatry

This book unearthed parts of my soul; drawing me to confront, heal, and grow. It reminded me that we walk a highway paved with challenges and triumphs, held together by the threads of faith, family, and grace.

Rev. Dr. Maxine Thomas
Founder and Executive Director of Sisters Keeping the Covenant

THAT LITTLE GIRL

MEMORIES, CHALLENGES, AND REFLECTIONS ON BLACK GIRL DREAMS

DR. CHARISSE L. GILLETT

Scripture quotations are from the New Revised Standard Version Bible.

Tehom Center Publishing is a 501(c)3 nonprofit publishing feminist and queer authors, with a commitment to elevate BIPOC writers. Its face and voice is Rev. Dr. Angela Yarber.

Paperback ISBN: 978-1-966655-23-7

Ebook ISBN: 978-1-966655-34-3

CONTENTS

To my parents, family and friends and the community that gave me space to be me.

FOREWORD

REV. SHEILA P. SPENCER

Sawubona

I see you.

Sawubona is an African greeting that translates to much more than the literal *I see you*. It carries a deeper meaning—it symbolizes recognizing the worth and dignity of another. It sees, affirms and acknowledges their journey, passions, strengths, struggles, and essence. *Sawubona* signifies offering full presence, letting the other person know they are deeply valued and truly seen.

It is the word that resonated in my spirit, body, and soul as I read *That Little Girl: Memories, Challenges, and Reflections on Black Girl Dreams*. The author truly says, *"I see you"* through every page.

Dr. Charisse L. Gillett is a mentor, friend, inspiration, Big Sister, colleague in ministry, and more. She is someone I admired from afar and, over the years, have been blessed to admire up close. She has always seen me—affirming, acknowledging, and lovingly calling out my gifts. Our lives have intersected in many ways, with each of us holding different roles. We know each other's families, and I've watched her children grow. But what I treasure most is that she has the beautiful ability to truly see the multifaceted parts of who I am. It is a rare gift when someone can see you through more than one lens—refusing to confine or define you by a single facet. She fully sees Sheila the educator, writer, administrator, the storyteller, the poet, and the minister. It is also the way that I see her.

Dr. Gillett embodies a rich, multifaceted life that cannot be defined or confined to one role. She is an educator, advocate, scholar, seminary president, and more. Within these pages, she is also a writer, a storyteller, and our guide. This book is a journey she takes us on—a journey where she sees all of us through her reflections. With each chapter, she invites us into her experiences, ending with a scripture and a blessing. *Sawubona*—she truly sees us.

She sees the beautiful Black girls who still dare to dream, reminding them that dreams do come true. She sees the ones who need to be reminded that it's okay *not to be okay*—that sometimes life is messy. She sees and recognizes us in the midst of life's messiness. Yet, as she so beautifully expresses, on the other side of messy, confusion, anxiety, and uncertainty, we can discover wisdom, support, and even a new version of ourselves.

She calls us to remember the lessons of the ancestors on whose shoulders we stand. The ancestors see us. I once read that in order for us to be born today, we needed a total of over 4,000 ancestors over the past 400 years. Dr. Gillett reminds us that they see us. She reminds us that we are the product of their prayers.

She invites us to see the gift of community—the family and friends who provide safe spaces for us to be vulnerable. She reminds us of our humanity, showing us that grief comes in many forms. She celebrates those who have carved out spaces of belonging. She acknowledges the moments when we must make decisions and take leaps of faith.

This treasure offers sacred reflections, life lessons, and lived experiences. Dr. Gillett invites us into her life journey and allows us to see both her and ourselves more clearly. She closes each chapter with a reflection and a prayer—a blessing to cover us as we journey onward.

In the tradition of *Sawubona*, when someone greets you with *"I see you,"* the response is *"Ngikhona—I am here."*

Through these pages, Dr. Gillett says, *"I see you."*

I invite our collective response to be, *"We are here."*

We are here to receive a book that makes us feel seen, held, and encouraged. I invite you into these sacred pages, where you, too, will find space to be fully seen, embraced, and affirmed—just as this book has done for me.

Thank you, Dr. Charisse L. Gillett, for saying yes to this journey. Thank you for showing us the little Black girl from Chicago who dreamed of writing a book—and did. On behalf of those who were waiting on the other side of your yes, we honor and celebrate this gift.

To be seen is to be loved.

To dream is to be free.

May this book remind every Black girl that she is both— deeply seen and endlessly free.

We Are Here,
Rev. Sheila P. Spencer

Educator | Spiritual Director | Minister | Speaker | Author |
Poet | Storyteller

www.sheilapspencer.com

ACKNOWLEDGMENTS

It's never done until it's done. I have heard a version of this all my life. It's never over until it's over. It's never done until I say it's done. As I write these acknowledgements, I hope that *That Little Girl* is finished! I want to be released to start my next project.

I am grateful for my husband who understood as I was working on this project that it did not involve a meeting, writing a sermon, reading a report, dinner preparations, or any activity for our granddaughter or children. I was not accessible. My time in my home office for nearly a year as I worked to finish this book was not about the kids, him, or the work that I love. Thank you, Donald K. Gillett, II for picking up the slack, for being you, and for your support.

I am grateful to my granddaughter Jayda, my children Jeremy, Liyah, Tasia and Trey for reminding me that we have much to talk about and for working towards ways to get to know and understand one another better. Our multi-layered relationships are a work in progress, but I trust God for the outcome and the increase.

Thank you, Vivian L. Brown, Natalie Green Houston, Donald K. Gillett, II, Jeremy Gillett, Carla Ross and Sharon E. Watkins for reading the early drafts of *That Little Girl* and affirming that some of what was on the pages of those early drafts might encourage and give hope to others. Thank you all for your encouragement to stick with it. Natalie, thank you for the introduction to Angela Tuck who read the second draft and offered to help me finish the project with an eye towards publication. Angela and I were not able to finish the project together but her advice to "fatten up" the manuscript and add more of me was sound.

I am grateful to Kris P. Bentley for introducing me to Eileen Campbell-Reed the host of the Writing Table. After listening to Kris praise the writing community she found around the Writing Table, and Eileen's help in moving her project forward, I finally sent her an email. It was a good decision. More than the insight and wisdom gained about storytelling, narrative and writing, Eileen offered me a way to shed the clinical language of reports and develop a creative discipline for writing *That Little Girl*. "Leave some breadcrumbs" was the best advice I received from her as a writer. Eileen's suggestion to write in small chunks every day has led me to this moment of celebration. It's done. I hope it's done, but if not, I can see the light at the end of the page. Thank you, Eileen Campbell-Reed.

Deep gratitude to the Kentucky Black Writers Collaborative and Claudia Love. My Black female voice and experiences felt affirmed when I attended the writers' conference, took a class taught by Eugenia Johnson Smith and participated in a "Burn The Mic" session in Midway, Kentucky. Claudia Love might have wondered why I kept showing up and why I was there that Sunday afternoon. We had met on several occasions. Perhaps she looked around the room that Sunday afternoon and saw a small group, so she was pleased to have another person in the room. I don't know.

What I do know is on that Sunday afternoon following church, I had planned to attend this "Burn the Mic" session and had put it on my calendar (evidence that I was serious). Despite the event being on my calendar, multiple efforts to derail my plans were presented by the universe. Refusing to cancel myself, I made it there. I wanted to experience other writers reading their creative work flowing from their spirit, heart, and intellect. My thinking was someday, I might have the opportunity to read something.

Looking at the group and realizing that someone did not show up, Claudia said to me, "You didn't sign up, but I know you have something to read." Then she said in a matter-of-fact way, "Don't be coy. Let's do this."

For the record, I am never coy. I wanted to do it, but I did not have anything with me because I had come from church. I did not have any drafts of my essays from *That Little Girl,* and I said to her, "I did not bring anything." She looked at me as if to say "coy!"

"Pull it up on your phone," she said. And so, I did. I shared the first public reading of "Dear Granny" at the "Burn the Mic" session in Midway, Kentucky. I heard finger snaps signaling appreciation. I heard *that's good* affirming some element of the essay. I heard a thoughtful *umm*. I left there thinking to myself, *keep going.*

Donald K. Gillett, II there is no way to thank you enough for being the husband I need in the relationship that works for us. We work because we work at being both/and. I am a wife and all the other things that make me. We allow one another to be a "me" and an "us" so that we can be who and what God has called each of us to be and do.

Thank you to all who allowed me to share that part of your life that intertwines with mine. In doing so I tried to speak in the voice of the girl that I was growing up, channeling my feelings, thoughts, and dreams. Finally, I am enormously grateful to my siblings and Dr. Sheila Saulsberry Morris for their love, care and friendship.

With hope,
Charisse Brown Gillett
November 2, 2024

PREFACE

I started this book shortly before the COVID-19 pandemic in response to a growing sense that my granddaughter and children did not understand the woman they saw daily in a black dress and pearls worn like a uniform. I felt a burning desire to ensure that these young people I was pouring myself into would know who was doing the pouring. Specifically, I've felt the need to tell my kids who I was in my life before I became the first lady, the minister, the president. As I watched my sons struggle with growing into their manhood and my granddaughter and daughters struggle with growing into their womanhood, I have heard them say to me *you don't understand*. As I tried to help, they dismissed the idea that I could be helpful. Our responses to one another were classic.

Thinking about it from their perspective of course a 50-plus-year-old woman could not understand their anxiety, their challenges, their unspoken hopes. I am not a person to them. I am not real to them. I am the taxi. I am the backup usher at church. I am that woman who does not understand who they were. They are the grandchild and children who do not understand the little girl who became their Grannymama and mother. My oldest son had more time with me, and he had a mother who was not a wife, minister, or president. He lived the journey, but he did not always know what motivated me. He only knew that I seemed determined to win, achieve, and do better no matter what. He remembered the table conversations surrounded by family and friends about each generation doing better than the last. He thought on some level that it was my acceptance of this historic responsibility to do better than my parents that drove me. I felt accountable to the sacrifices of my ancestors.

My oldest son thought it was my desire to make my parents proud, which motivated me. And, on some level, he was correct. That was part of what motivated me. Revisiting memories of my life as a kid reminded me of how difficult some periods of my life felt. It reminded me of my parents and siblings who knew me better than I knew myself. It reminded me of the people in my life who made room for the little girl who did not have it all together but certainly tried to make it look that way.

Revisiting my memories made it possible for me to understand more deeply my family, my choices and the grace and blessings that I have experienced on my journey. This book is for my children and granddaughter who think I don't "get it." This book is also for me, because I never want to forget the me of my childhood and teenage years. It's an ode to the memory of a little girl and teenager with dreams. I can only hope that my granddaughter and children read it and know that their Mama and Grannymama was once a little girl with dreams. Perhaps as they keep going, they will realize with the passage of time, hard work, good luck, and faith the journey is worth it in the end.

Charisse Brown Gillett
June 25, 2020

1

THAT LITTLE GIRL: ME

With each birthday, I find myself asking, "Did that really happen?" Perhaps, I dreamed those events in my little girl's imagination of what it was like to be me as a child. Did I overhear conversations and make up stuff to fit with my understanding of the facts and circumstances? I admit I wasn't sure and full of this uncertainty, off I would go to explore my memory through the memories of aunts, uncles, cousins, and siblings who shared such experiences with me. Did we really live in E-ville and walk around the corner to Granny's house? Did we really visit Nap-town and hang out with our cousins on Riverside Drive and sneak into the golf course at night? Did my cousin teach me how to swim at the neighborhood pool? Did we move from Robert Taylor Homes because gang members approached our Dad and said, "he's with us" (meaning our brother was with them)?

In searching for confirmation, I found that my memories were mostly correct. Yes, these events occurred, but those who shared the experience sometimes experienced the events differently and said events carried a different meaning for them. Exploring my memories about the who, what, where, when and how of my life and confirming those memories at a base level is important but for me what is more important is remembering the freedom of being a child. The memories of being a child experiencing life with laughter, joy and hope and allowing those memories to push themselves into the forefront of my existence with remembrances of my grand-mothers, aunts, and cousins all cascading into one large remembrance of me. Cascading into memories of being a kid.

I remember the smell of the places I lived as a child, the hard edges of voices through floor vents, car rides at night, and buses stalled in city traffic. I remember moving from a three-bedroom apartment without a yard to a five-bedroom house with a big yard and then back again. Each move brought with it new teachers, new friends, new enemies, and this also meant I was once again the new kid. I remember what it meant to be afraid and what it meant to be comforted by my parents and held by my sisters and brothers in hope.

I remember growing up when there were six of us, two boys and four girls. Then suddenly there was another baby. I wondered where did she come from? The new baby stayed downstairs with Mama. We slept upstairs.

My sisters and I are all piled up and tangled in the sheets of our big, shared bed. The fan is trying to encourage a breeze, but it's not working. Hot is HOT during a Chicago summer, just as Cold is COLD in winter. On this summer day none of us want to get up.

We hear voices downstairs and smell the bacon, but we don't care. We know it's the signal to get up, eat, and help cut the grass. It's a big yard and we did not finish it all yesterday. So again, we must get up, help cut the grass, rake the grass, and bag the grass. It's all about the grass and pulling weeds until the yard looks good.

The light is coming through a crack in the curtains. I peak one eye open and try to tell if anyone else is awake. Turning my head, I realize there is a foot nearly in my mouth. I smell my sister's skin, and it smells like the grass we helped to cut yesterday. My hand reaches out above me and my hand touches my other sister's hair. It feels soft and kinky-curly between my fingers and smells like Queen Bergamot hair grease. Both sisters feel a bit sticky and warm in the bed and in a room without air and one fan, but it's time to get up.

I push my younger sister to the edge of the bed to see if she is awake.

"Stop pushing me," she says.

"You need to go to the bathroom," I say.

"You go. I am going to stay here," she says.

"No. You go," I say.

"I do not need to do much to just cut grass. You go." She stays put.

I push my older sister. She heard the conversation and says, "Go. Don't go. Leave me alone."

I get up and go to the bathroom knowing the boys did not care about bathroom time. I remember wishing we had more than one upstairs bathroom for kids and one downstairs bathroom for Mama and Daddy.

Memories of my siblings as kids help me to remember me. Such memories help me to remember discovering what music I liked when I listened to WJPC, WLS and WGN on the radio. It helps me to remember a TV with five channels and an antenna like rabbit ears. It helps me to remember when all nine of us lived in a house together trying to get dressed with two bathrooms and meals cooked by mom. It even helps me to remember *me* when I think about the absence of male voices and a dad and brothers who left home only to return on holidays. I remember playing school with dolls and stuffed animals as my students. Of course, I was the teacher. I remember *a me* that was not a mom, Grannymama, employee, or wife.

I remember a me that had Black girl dreams. Sometimes I wondered if Black girls could have dreams. I did. I dreamed I would write a book. I practiced writing my book as a diary and then later as a journal of "my important thoughts." I practiced my interviews with Phil Donahue. But the book never came.

There was never enough time between this class or that meeting to write. Later there was never a time between the bills, the overdrawn checking account, or feeding a table full of hungry kids to think, let alone write. There was never enough time between the reports, the hyper scrutiny of my work, and the much-needed overtime to think, much less to write anything down. As it turns out, I've discovered at fifty-eight the story that I need to tell is the story of a teenager thinking about suicide. The story I need to tell is not the one of that of a mom trying to keep it together, or of a young wife balancing her ambitions with that of her husband, or a woman who became a president.

The story I need to tell is the story of a confused young girl who said to a friend. *I think I'm going to kill myself. I want to kill myself.*

There I said it. There I told you. There it is.

I've found evidence from that young woman who whispered to a friend "I want to kill myself." She is here today. I carried the anguish of those moments with me for a long time. I felt ashamed of my weakness. I tried to forget the words. I tried to forget the feelings of helplessness. I tried to forget the terror of that moment.

Swallowed by uncertainty, fear, ambition, dreams, despair, and depression, I whispered to a friend, "I want to kill myself."

It felt overwhelming. I was an ordinary young woman

struggling to make sense of boys, schoolwork, my parents' divorce, and the life stretching out ahead of me. I was well loved and thought I felt good about me. But somehow in that period of my life I became overwhelmed by the expectations placed upon me and the expectations I placed upon myself. My memories of this period in my life are filled with moments of coming home from school and work, going to my room and crying and crying. The pressure I felt was real, and the deadness I felt inside was scary. It was so messy in my head that I could not think of who to turn to for help. My mom. No. My Dad. NO! My siblings. No. I just could not find my way out of the mess that was in my head. I wanted to say something, but when I did, it came out as mush.

I was that little girl.

Reflection

Seek the Lord and God's strength; Seek God's presence continually.

—I CHRONICLES 16:11

The story I was telling myself in my head was messy. The life I was experiencing as that little girl was messy. I have learned with time and experience that life is messy. In fact, as I think about it and pray about it, I have come to accept that life is always a bit messy. Yet on the other side of messy, on the other side of confusion, on the other side of anxiety, on the other side of uncertainty, I found wisdom, support, and a new me.

My prayer for you is that on the other side of your messy, on the other side of the fog in your brain, on the other side of the confusion in your life, you reach for and have others who will give you the strength to understand and believe that today's messy can change. I am praying for you now. I am praying for the Spirit and strength of God to find its way into your spirit. I am praying that you find your priest and make your messy confession.

2
BLACK GIRL DREAMS

C an a little Black girl have dreams? I surely did. I had
dreams. Not just dreams of writing a book. I had
other dreams, too. But I wasn't sure how to make
those dreams come true. I dreamed that I could be Peggy Fair,
the office manager on the television show Mannix. Peggy was
played by Emmy-award winning actress, Gail Fisher. The
character Peggy Fair seemed to be in charge. She was the first
person visitors saw when they entered the office. She was the
one who went into Mannix's office to give him the details
about the visitor's problem. Mannix spoke to her with
respect, asked her opinion, and when he was out in the field
trying to resolve the episode's mystery, he called Peggy to
research the missing piece of information. Peggy always had
the answer or a suggestion that helped to solve the week's
mystery. Peggy had her own apartment, car, money, and she
was fashionably dressed. Peggy Fair was a woman with
choices. Whatever my dreams were, I wanted choices. And I
was deeply afraid I would not have them.

Busyness was the antidote to my fears in high school. The
busier I was the less time I had to think about my own hopes

and dreams and the emptiness inside of me. The less time I had to think about what I should do to stop the endless whirling around in my head. I tried to think about school and my job at Marshall Field & Company, an upscale department store in downtown Chicago. I tried not to think about my boyfriend. A great guy and a tall glass of water. He was also a source of some of my confusion.

He talked about marriage and life after high school as if we were destined to be together. I never thought of it... our being boyfriend and girlfriend that way. It was not my desire to be married. My Dad's mantra was: *Go to college. Get your own stuff. Know how to pay your own bills. Wait.*

My mom was clear. *Grow up first, but I can't stop you if that's what you want.* I was mad at my Dad at this point in my life, so I did not want to agree with him. I wanted my mom to say no but she understood that saying no was a guarantee that I would go in the opposite direction. All this to say, I drifted into an engagement thinking *maybe this won't work out after all.*

To have kids and live happily ever after...did not seem possible. The very mention of it made my flesh crawl. Hiding my feelings was part of the silent scream in my head. In fact, hiding how I felt was kind of second nature. Although my sisters and brothers and I were close, and you could see and feel how much we loved and protected each other, our sibling love also meant that each of us had to figure out how to hold our own. In a family of seven with so many voices, during endless debates, and with a challenge to every thought or idea, and in all the shouting to get a word in, it felt hard to be heard. It felt hard to be seen and hard to be understood. Sure, we all gathered around the table and shouted to make our points, but in our house every thought was challenged. In all that shouting and talking, I could hide.

When I thought about it, I did not really know any happily married couples. I knew plenty of divorced couples including my parents and several of their friends. And I knew plenty of unhappily married couples including the parents of some of my friends. I stopped hanging out at their houses because the tension when both parents were home was thick. I knew unmarried unhappy couples. From my high school perspective, I was watching a lot of married and unmarried adults pretending to be happy. I saw them whispering to each other. Sometimes I would hear loud voices, slamming doors, and then the TV would get louder to cover the arguing and fighting. Love did not look like much fun to me, and the constant talking about the love stuff wore on me. The pressure to have sex, to be coupled up, and to pretend that was what life was all about, made me hide how I felt. I thought, *what is the big deal?*

In Romeo and Juliet, the lovebirds died. In Westside Story, the lovebirds died. But in Claudine the movie, the heroine, played by Tony-award winning actress Diahann Carroll, was smart. She was tough. She loved her kids. And she didn't die. But life was hard. I was terrified that I would give in to some unspoken expectation that I should get married, have babies, and get a job. I wanted to go to college, but I did not have any money, and I did not know how to go about it. The get married, get a job, and have a baby thing? I was sure someone could help me do, but *Oh my God that couldn't be the life I was going to live... could it?*

Dreaming about how to escape the graduate-from-high-school-and-get-married trap created an internal anxiety that led me to pretend it was all okay but inside there was a fog. The fog seems to grow and get darker and darker with each day. School, the French Club, the school newspaper, the Junior and Senior Prom committees, and my job at the local Marshall Field & Company kept me busy and moving forward. My second job came as an Andy Frain Usher, a professional ushering and security service founded in

Chicago. Working as an Andy Frain Usher introduced me to more choices. It took me to the ballet and symphony at Orchestra Hall and to live concerts and theatre at the Arie Crown and Goodman Theatres.

Everything felt overwhelming. Even with school, work, and family filling my time, I still felt emptiness and confusion inside. The feelings were real. I was never sure of what to do. I might have looked alright on the outside but on the inside, it felt like one big messy jumble.

Jumble or not, after I graduated from high school, I took the Greyhound Bus to Iowa City to live with my Dad for the summer before moving to Cedar Falls to go to college. I applied late for school. I had no money. I did not know what to do or how to do it, but I went. Iowa was not Los Angeles, and I was not Peggy Fair. I was me. I was determined. I held onto my dreams, and I delayed children and marriage until after college. I held onto to that little girl who wanted more choices and dreamed more dreams.

Reflection

I can do all things through Christ who strengthens me.

— PHILIPPIANS 4:13

To have dreams at all as a little Black girl is to make a statement about your life. I was making a statement that I mattered. I wanted to be somebody a la Jesse Jackson's "I am somebody" mantra, which I saw on Saturday morning Operation PUSH (People United to Save Humanity) broadcast on WJCP. I wanted to *be* whatever that meant, and I felt I had something to offer. I was dreaming, and I made choices that I thought enabled my dreams. In my awkward often clumsy fashion, I pushed towards unspoken, and half formed dreams just to *be*. I did not do it alone. I now know my Aunt Armetta and Uncle Stephen prayed for me and my siblings as we grew up in the big city. They prayed that God would strengthen those around us so that we would be safe, be courageous, and someday be able to seek God's will for our lives.

My prayer for you is that you dream dreams that will take you to the moon. I pray that you know in this moment someone is praying that the dreams you carry in your secret place will someday have space to grow and flourish in ways that you can *be*.

3

DEAR GRANNY

I hate being late. I just hate it!

On the day of Granny's funeral, we arrived an hour early at New Hope Missionary Baptist Church as directed. And yet we were "late." The main parking lot and the overflow parking were filled to capacity, and all nearby street parking was taken. We should have planned to show up at least *two hours* early if we wanted to park near the church and avoid walking two or three blocks in heels. There were a lot of Browns and Brown kinfolk who lived in town who would know better than to show up an hour early to Granny's service and think that would be enough time to park, fellowship with church members, and catch up with family. But here we were, some of her family walking into an already crowded church house…late.

Granny was a Mother of the Church. She was well loved and respected by her church and the community. The headline in the local newspaper read, "A Solider for the Church has gone home to be with the Lord." She helped to start the church's Pantry of Hope. She mentored young women. And

Granny taught me and other young church goers how to tithe. "Always give the Lord his due," she said.

Now I was walking into Granny's funeral. I was having a hard time processing that she was gone. As I began encountering guests, I had a hard time responding truthfully to their questions about my feelings. Mostly I wished the probing would stop, and we could all admit the obvious. Today was hard. We were putting our best foot forward. Full stop.

Honestly, we probably showed up only an hour before the service because I did not want to hug and kiss and chat and laugh before the service. I did not want to hear the obligatory, "She's in a better place with the Lord."

And, I did not want to have to say, "Yes, she's with the Lord. She has her room in God's mansion." I was afraid if I spent too much time fellowshipping, catching up, and hugging strangers who loved my Granny, then my composure would fail. I might fall out on the floor wailing like a baby. In truth, I was grateful we were "late." I was relieved that we only had time for a few hugs and brief conversations before the procession into the service with our family.

The eulogist said, "Eugenia preached her own funeral." I came out of my fog and thought, *Really? Granny must preach her own funeral? Can't you do that? Even in death does this woman have to stand up and account for herself? If she's looking down on us today, surely, we can give her flowers.*

I came out of my fog again when my cousin Vince offered words of thanks for our Granny. He talked about her faith, her love of her family, her willingness to give the last of everything to everyone. He talked about the secret candy dish of spearmint and orange fruit jellies in the cabinet behind the back door. He talked about our Granny who made each of us feel like we had hung the moon in the sky. *And this is the woman,* I thought, *who has to preach her own funeral?* I knew the language was a way of recognizing that Granny had lived a life worthy of her faith, but still it set my teeth on edge. Today, she should not have to lift a finger.

When my Uncle Stephen, known to others as the Rev. Stephen Brown, approached me following the repast, saying he wanted to talk with me, I felt certain he was going to take time to assure me that his mother was with the Lord and no longer suffering. I could hear the words before he said them. "Charisse, your Granny, my mother, is with the Father now. She is where she belongs. She was a good Christian, and she is in a Heavenly place so don't worry about your Granny. She's fine. She's finc."

Uncle Stephen was passionate and my favorite Uncle. But the Rev. Brown was something else. I loved him, yet I wasn't sure I had it in me to listen today. He was capable of preaching, evangelizing, and witnessing to anyone anywhere including witnessing to his niece at the repast of his mother. I smiled and readied myself for what I knew was going to be a long conversation.

Instead, he handed me an envelope tucked inside a Bible. The letter was addressed to Granny. Uncle Stephen said, "This was in Granny's Bible. I thought you would want it back." The letter was written and sent by me.

On the ride home I looked at the unexpected envelope wondering what my 17-year-old self might share with my 38-year-old self about grieving the loss of her Granny.

September 27, 1979

Dear Gran,

Every so often I get really <u>depressed.</u> I don't even know why or if I do, I will not admit it to myself. It's not a good thing to cry for no reason.

I don't know where this feeling comes from; only that I really want to get rid of it. The other night I read a feature story that said reach for and take your stars. Make what you have work for you. I'm so scared I will not or cannot reach my stars. It's driving me mad. At school everyone thinks I'm the girl who has it all or is doing everything to gain everything that seems to be important in my young life. I feel pressured by my own sense of 'I must be the best or nothing.' I don't know where this feeling comes from; only that I want to get rid of it.

School is a daily reminder of how intelligent I am supposed to be. So why do I doubt this rather obvious intelligence? I'm starting to think I'm not so smart, I'm not that bright. I'm wishing people wouldn't always say this is so. I don't think it is true. I talked to Uncle Steven about going to college but I'm not even sure that's what I want. I know money is a chief factor in this decision, but even if the money was here do I want to go to college and possibly fail all my classes? This is not the most positive attitude, but it is the only one I have. I know Mama and Daddy would be disappointed if I didn't go but I'm not even sure what I would study.

My interests are so wide. I feel like I am only half as good at the things I do. Granny, please understand that this letter is one I want to be between you and me only. I don't think Daddy or Mama would understand. They would only think I am crazy, which I am not.

Give all my love and tell Uncle Steven I am trying to gain peace of mind and put my values in the correct order.

Love, Charisse Brown

Reflection

She opens her mouth with wisdom, and the teaching of kindness is on her tongue.

— PROVERBS 31:26

I almost forgot I wrote this letter to my Granny. When I reread it, I remember that little girl. I remember how much I trusted my grandmother to hear me, to really listen to me and give me good advice. I trusted her to guide me as I had seen her do so many times with my cousins and members of her church. I trusted her with my insecurities. She remembered me and loved me to the very end of her life, and her care gave me what I needed even in my grief. Sometimes it is the faith of our mothers that lifts us up. She prayed for me. She got down on her knees and prayed for me.

Thank you, Granny, for living a life of prayer and love that nurtured, nourished, and held me even to this day.

Sheila, Chicago

4

THAT LITTLE GIRL: A PRIEST

Some things I don't want to remember. It's been so long ago that I tried not to remember that it happened. It's been so long ago that I could almost pretend it didn't happen. Because of the passage of time, I could pretend that little girl did not exist. If I wanted to, I could pretend that young woman was gone forever.

Except there is evidence of her existence. That little girl is always there lurking in the relationships and conversations with my sisters and my childhood friends. She shows up on every trip home. While lingering over a meal or doing the dishes, the "do you remember so-and-so" part of the family visit would begin.

Then someone would say Sheila's name. At first, I would pretend not to hear the question or statement. After all who could hear anything in Mama's house full of people with music and the TV going? Never mind all the grand kids running around. Sometimes I could pretend I was answering questions about *our* Sheila (our youngest sister's name is Sheila). On Thanksgiving my sister Sheila heard me answer a question about her that was not about her. She said, "Girl what's wrong with you? You know she's not talking about me!" Busted! I could not pretend I had not heard the questions or that I was responding in error. There it was. *Girl, what's wrong with you?* The *wrong with me* was if I remembered my friend Sheila, then I had to remember *me*.

My sisters and I met Sheila one day when she was walking in front of our house. Our unruly dog Poochie barked and hopped around, looking for all the world as if he would attack her. She had a paper bag in her hand and started to breathe into the bag. I thought it was strange... someone breathing into a bag!

Sheila became a friend to us, like the sixth sister in the Brown family. We played together, talked each day, shared meals, and secrets. We thought she had asthma, which sort of explained the paper bag. I also learned when it counted, she was a compassionate listener, a minister, and she heard my confessions.

So, years later when I sort of misunderstood questions or was fuzzy on some memories. I should not have been surprised when our sister, Sheila, called me out on it. It was never going to work. We all remembered our sixth sister and our ongoing friendship, the house parties, the closeness. It was easy to call BULLSHIT. And I was forced to remember my priest. Yes, my priest, Sheila, my friend who was two years younger than me. I was also forced to remember our conversation.

It was an afternoon after school. I called my friend Sheila, and I said, "You home?"
She said, "I just got home. What's up?"
I could not get the words out, so I hung onto the phone.
"Hey Risse. What's up?"
Still the words would not come out of my mouth.

Finally, Sheila whispered, "Are you okay? I mean okay, okay? Did something happen?"

"Nothing happened," I whispered. "I think I want to kill myself."

The moments following this desperate whisper are hazy. What I remember are the quick questions Sheila asked me.

"Hey, you, okay?"

"Yeah."

"Hey, how was school?"

"Good."

"Hey, you, okay?

"Yeah."

Finally, she said, "Why are you so sad?"

Why? I wondered.

"I don't know. I really don't know."

"Risse, I'm praying for you. I'm praying for you. I'm praying for you."

My minister was not the pastor of the local church or my uncle or the pastor who lived around the corner. The minister, priest, and pastor who heard and held the confession of my fragile young self was a beautiful young woman two years younger than me. She was funny, happy, and compassionate. I told her my secret. *I want to kill myself.*

She believed my desperate whisper. She may have had asthma, and needed a paper bag to control her breathing, but she was able to breathe with me through my scariest thoughts. She walked with me until I could see the light.

Decades later, I called her and asked, "Do you remember when we were girls."

"Yes."

"Do you remember what I said? What we did?"

"Yes."

"Thank you for taking me seriously. I did not know what to do. I did not understand why I was feeling that way. I just felt overwhelmed and blurted the words out. *It felt real.*"

"It sounded real to me Risse, and all I knew to do was to talk to you, and to pray with you, and to pray for you."

I am forever grateful God put her in my path. On that day and in that moment, God introduced me to my minister. She was that little girl.

Reflection

Then suddenly the Lord you are seeking will come to the temple; the messenger of the covenant whom you desire will come says the Lord Almighty.

— MALACHI 3:1

My prayer for you is to recognize the priest, the pastor, the friend that God sends to you in the midst of your struggles. Recognize the genuine spirit of God's messenger in the words of encouragement, in the tears, and in the promise to stand with you. Strip away the robes, the titles, and the grandiose prayers and really see who God is sending to you spirit-to-spirit. I will send my messenger, who will prepare the way before me.

Carlos, Crystal, Cathy, Carla, Charisse, Clayton & Sheila
Mom's College Graduation, Riverdale, IL

Mom & Me
East Second Street Christian Church

Mom and Me,
High School Graduation

5
MOM

There's no way I can pay you back. But the plan is to show
you that I understand. You are appreciated.

— TUPAC SHAKUR, "DEAR MAMA" (1985)

As a child I did not know her very well. I did not
have a sense of her hopes and dreams for her life,
nor did I really understand the woman she had
become. It was not until I heard my mom's sisters talk about
her as *their sister* that I realized my mom was someone other
than *my mom*.

When my Aunt Linda talked about her sister Vivian, she
talked about how determined her sister was to learn how to
play the clarinet in elementary school. When my Aunt Lillian
talked about her sister Vivian, she talked about how much
she enjoyed being in the marching band.

"Where the marching band went so did your mom. Your
mom wanted to see and explore the world," said Aunt Linda.

"Your Mama dreamed she would become a nurse, a
teacher, or a TV analyst," said her older sister Lillian.

When my aunts talked about my mom, they described a woman I did not know. Their sister was smart, funny, determined, beautiful, fashionable, and sexy. This woman who was my mom had hopes and dreams that came before me and did not include me. She had beautiful shiny black hair, large brown eyes, and a wide smile. She loved matching shoes and purses. As a little girl, I would sneak into her room and try on her clothes, and she knew it.

"Charisse," she said, "stay out of my things!"

"Mama, it wasn't me. It wasn't me. It was Carla."

"It was you and now you are lying on your sister. It was you and you stretched my sweater out of shape. Stay out of my things, Charisse."

"Yeah, Risse she knows it was you because your shoulders are so big they mess up our clothes and stretch them out of shape. *Stop lying on me,*" said Carla.

I had no defense. So, I said, "Shut up, Carla."

Mom clearly felt exasperated about the sweater, but with five daughters she was accustomed to us trying on her clothes, playing with her shoes, and spraying her perfume. It was my attempt to blame my sister that ticked her off. My mom and my sisters had small frames and stood 5'3" to 5'5" in heels and they weighed in around 120 to 130 pounds. I was 5'7" and 150 pounds, and I had big shoulders. The truth was easy to figure out, and there was nothing to lie about.

The woman who became my mom was warm, sweet, and determined. I loved the way she smelled like the spices she used to cook with and Estee Lauder Perfume in the blue bottle. I remember my mom in her role as mother. She got me up in the morning. She had breakfast on the table. Sometimes it was hot Malt-O-Meal or Cream of Wheat in the cold Chicago winter. It was bacon and eggs in the summer and spring. She sat on the porch and watched us play in the playground below and watched us walk home from school. She protected us.

When Robert Taylor Homes turned into a battleground for rival gangs, she never let us out of her sight. When watching us was no longer enough, she got a job so that she and my Dad could buy a home with enough bedrooms and baths for a family of nine. In our new home she sat on the porch and watched us until she was sure this new home was safe, not safer than what we had left but safe. Full stop.

When the new home, new job, new clothes, and new car weren't enough to fill the gaps in our parents' relationship, she left. And she took us with her. I remember the years after the separation and divorce. She was strong. She worked to pay bills. We listened to Sam Cooke's "Bring it On Home to Me," Aretha Franklin's, "Respect" and "Chain of Fools," Shirley Caesar's "Don't Drive Your Mama Away", and Andraé Crouch's "Jesus is the Answer." She filled out papers for this program or that field trip so we could participate in activities at school. She studied for her degree. She taught us to be smart about who we chose as friends. And why we were with them. She was my mother, not the Vivian that her sisters Lillian, Linda, and Griselda knew.

I met Vivian-with-the-dreams when I was a senior in high school. That Vivian came home one day with books and a schedule from the local community college and announced, "I'm going to college, too." She had worked and guided seven teenagers into young adulthood. Then she decided it was time for her to go back to school. She finished her associate of arts degree while I was in my sophomore year of college graduating with her oldest daughter Carla and her sister Linda in the same ceremony!

Several years later, she completed her Bachelor of Business Administration at 55 years of age using a tuition wavier benefit from her daughter's employer. Her seven children, sisters, mother-in-law, and friends attended the ceremony. Despite the pleas from the graduation platform, we all joined in with shouts of joy and celebration. We shouted "Vivviannn! Vivviannn! Mama! Mama!" Our shouts said, "Give us a break. You don't know the trouble she's seen. You don't know the blessing she is. You don't know what this woman has done. Mama!"

There were hard days and there were times of laughter and joy. There were head strong kids. And daughters who knew everything. There were sons who tested the boundaries of life and an ex-husband who frustrated her. At 17 I would cry myself to sleep. I cried deep hard sobs. She would come to my room, pat me on the back and say, "It will be okay. It will be okay. Not today, but someday."

To this day I don't know why I could not talk with her about my inner life, but I could not. Perhaps I did not want to add to her plate. Perhaps, I did not want to interrupt her again as she tried to reach for a life after raising seven kids. I don't really have that answer. What I do know is that my mom made choices that I can now see and understand. She was helping to shape and frame, not only her life, but my life for the better.

Her straightforward, "Stay out of grown folks' business!" was a response to my anger at my Dad following their separation and divorce. I understand her words better now. My Dad was not her husband. My Dad was my Dad. She was clear about that, and she taught me also to be clear. I learned how to be responsible for the decisions that I made – good or bad. I learned how to face my mistakes and to self-correct to avoid certain disaster. I learned how to love my children through our mutual discomfort. I learned how to mother my children because my mother loved and mothered me.

Later in life mom faced one health challenge after another. She tried hard not to be limited by those challenges. She found a way around the problem or through it. Her determination to live life, to enjoy life, reminds me of the Tim McGraw song, "Live Like You Were Dying." The song is an anthem to a life reconsidered and to the person fighting to live that life with grace, joy, courage, and passion in the face of enormous health challenges. It is a story about meeting a man whose remaining life is short. This song and especially these lyrics speak to me.

> *How's it hit ya, when you get that kind of news?*
> *Man, what'd ya do? And he said,*
> *I went sky divin'*
> *Rocky Mountain climbin'*
> *I went 2.7 seconds on a bull named Fu Manchu.*
> *I loved deeper*
> *And I spoke sweeter*
> *And I gave forgiveness I'd been denying.*

Tim McGraw sings with passion and a bittersweet hope that all of us will get the chance to live with such abandonment. He hopes people will have another chance to get it right and mend the fences that need to be mended. On more than one occasion I found myself blasting this song in the car or while I'm working out. It made me think of my mom and appreciate her strength.

My mom lived with fullness in the years, months and days left to her following a diagnosis of renal failure. She found the strength to live following the death of a daughter and a son. I saw her attend her granddaughter's college graduation and sit in the front row as that granddaughter gave the commencement address. She beamed with pride when her grandson received a standing ovation for his acting and responded to questions about his artistic choices as a playwright. I saw her attend her grandson's graduation from an

Ivy League school where he received his PhD. I saw her celebrate her daughter's 60th birthday waving balloons, dancing, and smiling into the camera. I saw her make room in her home for grandchildren as they explored young adulthood. She took the Mega Bus to Kentucky to celebrate her grandchildren in Easter Sunday Church programs, flew to Texas to witness high school and college graduations, helped a grandson with homework on the weekends in Chicago as his mother worked the third shift. She loved the adventure of traveling on the Mega Bus to see her family. My mom had a calendar and scheduled annual visits to see her kids and grandchildren. She spent Thanksgiving in Chicago. She made trips to Texas, Kentucky, Indiana, and California each year.

Ten years after learning to live with a diagnosis of renal failure, Mom fell. She had been in the hospital, then the rehab center. Finally at home for a few months, she was learning to trust her body and to walk again. For a woman who was always on the go, this was difficult. In the wake of so many days of being cooped up in the house, she reached her limit!

"Get me out of this bed. Get me out of this house," she said. With the help of my sisters and brother, she got settled in the motorized wheelchair. Once comfortable, she took a second to relearn the controls. Then she put my sister's dog Fluffy on her lap and took off. She pushed the button down on the arm of the wheelchair and took off down the street saying, "Fluffy, we are going for a ride, and I am driving!"

Mom went wheel chairing on a beautiful sunny day with Fluffy sitting on her lap. They went up the street and around the corner with mom managing the remote on the wheelchair in 5.2 minutes. We were scared that the wheelchair would hit a crack in the sidewalk and both mom and Fluffy would get hurt when the wheelchair crashed. But none of that happened. Mom managed the wheelchair. Fluffy was calm on her lap, and we walked behind her down the block and around the corner, returning home with no mishaps and a happy and satisfied Mom.

"I got out of this house. I had to get out of this house," she said.

Once again, my mom showed us how to live and reach for life with both hands.

Reflection

Honor her for all that her hands have done, and let her works bring praise at the city gate.

— PROVERBS 31:31

I really met Vivian, a woman who was more than a mom, when I saw her reaching for her dreams and showing me as a young woman how not to give up and discard my dreams. She showed me how to work for my dreams and believed that the next day would be better. I began to understand Vivian as I watched her live with news that could have taken her hope and joy for living. Yet she continued to live and reach for life regardless of the challenges. I was the daughter of that strong woman. My mom was that little girl. I was that little girl. She is the woman who loved and mothered me into me.

Jeremy, Jayda, Liyah, Tasia, and Trey, Fall 2020

6

THE STRUGGLES ARE REAL

If they hadn't told me I was ugly, I never would have searched for my beauty. And, if they hadn't tried to break me, I wouldn't know that I am unbreakable.

— GABOUREY SIDIBE (MAKERS CONFERENCE, 2018)

"Which one is it today?" I asked my husband. I was asking which of the girls had come home from school crying. It had become a regular part of our routine. Once or twice a week one of the girls would come home upset and sometimes outright sobbing. Was it freshman, sophomore, or junior? The freshman was struggling to find the right peer group but liked track. She has been practicing in hopes of making the team. I was hoping it was not her. The sophomore was starting a new job and had trouble sometimes holding her tongue. This was her third job, and we wanted her to keep it because it was around the corner from our home, and she could get there by taking low traffic roads. I was hoping it was not her because I wanted this job to work out. The junior, our granddaughter was a third-year cheerleader and had a game tonight, which I had no energy to coax her into attending. I was tired and was not sure I could mother any of them tonight.

My question was premature. My husband met me at the door to tell me he was on his way out of town for a tournament with our youngest son.

"No tears today!" he told me.

I couldn't believe it. No Friday night tears because of some crazy remarks hurled at one of my girls by a teenage tormentor, coach, or teacher? No need to get ready for an unscheduled Monday morning parent-teacher conference because one of my girls refused to let someone call them a B. Not my girls. In their best Queen Latifah voice, I taught them to say, "who you callin' a B?" Often, I braced myself for a comprehensive drama report. In this age of cell phones, Facebook, selfies, photo bombs, snapchat, mean girls, and cruel boys, one of our three girls came home often wrestling with the pain caused by the day.

"They said I was ugly," said my youngest daughter.

"Who are *they*?" I asked. "And what do *they* know?"

"They said I was fat," said my oldest daughter.

"Who are *they*?" I asked.

"They said I shouldn't be in AP classes, and the coach said my hair was messy," said my granddaughter.

"Who are *they*? What do *they* know?"

It was a weak response. I knew it. They knew it. But I kept pleading with them to see what I saw. I kept trying to get them to understand that the messy jumble that is being a teenager was on some level just a process of growing up. I also told them that being a young Black girl is difficult because the beauty that is *within you* and the beauty that *is you* is not celebrated.

"I want you to believe in your own intellect regardless of

what others say." I told them. "And a beautiful healthy body is better than the alternative."

"Okay, Mama, stop preaching."

"We get it."

"Okay, Granny, I got it. We are smart. I'm smart. Yeah. Ok."

The struggle is real I thought. What do you say to kids and a granddaughter struggling with unspoken judgements of society, self-love, boys, abandonment issues, self-worth, fear, and everyday teenage hormones? What do you do when your kids and granddaughter try to navigate an onslaught of daily negativity? I lived it. I remember it. Keep going. It will get better. Another weak response but I said it anyway.

Our youngest son was not there yet. There was still an innocence to his face and in his smile. Nonetheless I knew the day was coming when the switch would be flipped. I could imagine it. Worse, I could feel the day when his teachers and the neighbors started to see him as something other than a young boy trying to make sense of his world. I could feel the day when his mistakes might define him in the eyes of others and opportunities could slip away.

I felt sad and angry that my kids and my granddaughter might not have the chance to make mistakes and learn from those mistakes. *For crying out loud, why can't they just go to school, be teenagers, and be themselves? Why can't Black kids make mistakes and recover?*

For years now, we have been telling each child that their dreams are possible. We try to encourage them. Yet, standing here on a Friday night, relieved that no one is crying, I could also imagine a complicated future for each one of my heartbeats.

I knew each one of them would likely confront internal and external battles to reach their dreams. I also knew each one of them would one day look at us, the grown folks in their lives who loved, encouraged, and protected them, as the enemy. On the one hand it's part of having the courage and strength to spread wings and fly. On the other hand, being Black and judged and criticized and compared to a white default was sometimes overwhelming. Their struggles to grow up in an anti-Black world are mixed up with the timeless adult-kid maturing issues. I imagine one day they will wonder if we protected them too much or outright lied. In the struggle they will doubt if hard work, education, support, mentors and a belief in God truly lead to the realization of their dreams. Having a front row seat to their struggles, sometimes I wonder if the dreams of my granddaughter, daughters and sons are less viable for them than mine were for me growing up on the southside of Chicago?

I also hope one day life will come full circle, and they will look back and know without any doubt that when we taught them to believe in themselves, to search for their own worth, to believe in a God of hope, and to claim their own values, they will know we offered this encouragement and love to help them survive and thrive in a world that did not believe in them. I hope they will know fully just how beautiful, beloved, and cherished they are. My heartbeats they remain.

Reflection

For surely I know the plans I have for you, says the Lord,
plans for your welfare and not for harm, to give you a future
with hope.

— JEREMIAH 29:11

My prayer for those who are bullied, for those who feel
inadequate for those who are hurting is to keep fighting for
the life you have and your unrealized dreams. Gather yourself and be fearless about living. Be fearless about seeking
medical help. My prayer for you is that you hang on until the
fog in your brain is gone. God really does love you and the
Creator has work for you to do.

7

FAKE MAMA: DON'T FORGET ME

This act of remembering is an important one to my own sense of vocation. In remembering, we recall those people who called us to life.

— PATRICK B. REYES, *NOBODY CRIES WHEN WE DIE* (2016)

Visits to the local community service office so our kids could spend time with their birth mother was an adventure. The adventure included visits arranged by a third party, our kids coming home in different clothes than they were wearing a few hours earlier. Then they needed a few days to readjust following each visit.

Life was already adventurous as busy professionals and as grandparents to a 3-year-old granddaughter. We provided support for her mother and our son as they tried to go to work, finish school, and be parents. The adventure became livelier when we became foster parents to a sibling group of three, ages six months, one-year-old, and two-years-old. Suddenly, our full but orderly life became a big messy adventure. There were four of everything. There were four car seats, four diaper bags, a house that smelled of formula, baby lotion, oatmeal, and poop. The adventure expanded when we decided to adopt the babies. We entered a two-year process of adoption.

Mandated by the court until the adoption process was complete, the visits to Monica who gave birth to all three foster children became a part of our monthly routine. The two little ones were oblivious to the occasion, but Big Girl understood something was changing. It was not until I overheard Monica talking to Big Girl that I understood what was happening. Big Girl started trying to do what her birth mom had told her to do, and not to see me as her mom.

I spoke quietly to my husband. "Honey," I said, "I heard Monica tell Big Girl, 'I am your real Mama. Tell your brother and sister I said so. These social workers are trying to take y'all from me. These people are trying to take y'all.'" She was looking Big Girl in her eyes and holding the child's face a few inches from her face. It was intense for a two-year-old. It was intense for me.

I mean, I think I heard those words from her. She was talking and whispering loudly. It seemed to be on purpose so I would hear, too. She said these words as she hugged her kids good-bye.

"Honey," I said to my husband, "Didn't you hear her? She kept saying to Big Girl, 'I am your real Mama.' And Big Girl looked confused and hurt."

"Look," he said to me, "I didn't hear her." We were getting into the car. He said, "Not in front of the kids. Let's get them home and talk about it later." I did not like his tone, but I knew he was right.

From the age of three and more intensely after the formal adoption, Big Girl woke up every day ready to resist me, like I was her "fake Mama." It was like she was ready to tell the

fake Mama, "You are not my Mama!" I wasn't. She understood, I was not her Mama, and she said so! As they got older
the other kids could be heard saying to Big Girl, "What is up
with you? She is nice. She is pretty. She smells good. She yells
and uses bad words like a Mama. She hugs and kisses us. She
does Mama-like things. She's a real Mama."

"She's a real Mama but she's not *our r*eal Mama. She's
fake," said Big Girl. Drop the mic!

Her feelings were deep. I recognized her sadness, tears,
refusal to cooperate, and anger as part of her loss and her
grief. But it pissed me off when I had to clean up literal poop
off the floor or toilet when she had an "accident" or when she
deliberately told the other kids not to follow my instructions.
They seemed confused about what to do. I got it, but I was
still extremely upset with the constant challenge.

Intellectually, it made sense to me. Big Girl was trying to
hang onto the woman who gave her life. But on the ground, I
was trying to manage four kids and my career. I was
supporting my busy husband who was also engaged in
ministry. Parenting, mothering and being a Grannymama was
hard. Concrete-driveway hard. There was no give in this little
girl, and sometimes there was no give in the other kids either.

She was holding onto those memories that gave her some
control of her life. She was holding onto a person in whose
face she could see herself reflected. She told me often, "my
Mama is gonna come get me." I knew she was holding out for
the day Monica would come back and get her. I also knew
that day was at least a decade into the future because we had
decided we could not co-parent or participate in an open
adoption with Monica. Before she would reunite with Monica
there would be parent-teacher conferences, school activities,
teenage hormones, Mama's menopause, boyfriends, and a lot
more. I wasn't sure how to get from point A to point B. But I
just kept parenting, loving, doing what needed to be done. At

some point over the years, I transitioned from being the "fake Mama," and I became the Mama. I just kept showing up for my kid fake Mama and all. I showed up.

I showed up by knocking on the bathroom door to check on her when she took too long, and the water ran too much. I showed up at school when it seemed as if school was becoming an obstacle course instead of a place for learning. I showed up at volleyball practice when it seemed like practice was becoming a place of ridicule. I did what I knew to do and that was to show up and keep trying until my Big Girl could at least reach for me when she needed me.

The back porch became our place for conversation. Sitting on that back porch listening to her, I heard in her voice the echoes of another young girl struggling to make sense of her world. That girl who wrote a letter to her Granny. That girl who shared a secret with her friend Sheila.

Big Girl called her Granny Vivian every night to talk and when Granny Vivian visited us, you could hear the two of them talking into the night. A Granny was what a young girl needed. She was struggling to make sense of an origin story laced with separation, heartache, and love. For a mother (me) who struggled to keep it together and learn how to talk with her daughter, a mother is what I needed, too. "Just listen to her. Stop trying to fix it. Just listen," said my Mom to me.

Out on the deck looking at the stars, we learned to talk to one another. We argued. I learned to hear Big Girl. We sat in angry silence sometimes. We sat in easy silence sometimes. We listened to music. We listened to Deniece Williams singing "Black Butterfly." At the top of our lungs, we would join in singing:

> *As the darkness gives way to dawn,*
> *You've survived...*
> *Black Butterfly*

Sail across the waters
Tell your sons and daughters
What the struggle brings

To my granddaughter I was a Grannymama who turned every conversation into a much needed "talk" laced with love and understanding. To Big Girl it sounded like empty words. To her it sounded like I was preaching. I had the words and the love, but the music made it plain for us and it helped fake Mama, and Big Girl reach for one another on the way to becoming mother and daughter.

Reflection

But those who wait for the Lord shall renew their strength; they shall mount up with wings like eagles; they shall run and not be weary; they shall walk and not faint.

— ISAIAH 40:31

Finding a way to love through the surprises and difficulty of mothering is not for the faint of heart. Loving is hard. Loving each other when we don't see and hear each other clearly is harder. My prayer for moms, daughters, Grannymamas, and sons is that you learn to really hear each other and learn to listen to one another's hopes, dreams, and desires. My prayer is that you learn to see yourselves in each other's experiences and love one another into a better relationship. There can be joy on the other side of it all.

Dad and Me, High School Graduation

8

THE BEST DADDY

I always knew when my dad was coming home. Before he arrived, the house would come alive. During the day, the coffee pot appeared on the stove. The smell of bacon would be in the air. Toast and jelly would appear on the table. At night, I would smell chicken, liver, or greens. It seemed like we would all start moving around because my mom started moving around. I was never aware of when he left, but the smell of food and my mom moving around the house no matter how early or late, was a sure sign that my dad was coming home. Those of us awake would run to the door and wait for him to enter the house.

Once he was inside, we waited until he took his place in the center of the living room. And he would say in a loud voice, "Who's the best Daddy in the whole wide world?"

We waited a beat and then we yelled in our loudest voices, "MY DADDY!"

These moments are some of the best memories I have of my dad.

"Charisse," he would say, "What have you done today?"

"I learned a new word," I answered.

"A new word. What word? What does it mean? Use it in a sentence." His questions came fast, and I learned to answer quickly.

His last question was always, "What do you want to be when you grow up?"

It was the question he asked of all seven of his children, even the baby. We had to have an answer. I think my baby sister started crying for her bottle when it was her turn to answer, but her cry was an answer.

We all *had* an answer. If one of us didn't have an answer, then the rest of us had to hear Dad telling us about how hard it is being Black in a world without a job, education, or money. The rest of us had to hear about doing better than the last generation. The rest of us had to hear about beauty being skin deep. We learned it was better to have an answer.

Then he would say again, "Who's the best Daddy in the whole wide world?"

We waited a beat and then yelled again in our loudest voices, "MY DADDY!"

These are enduring memories of my dad. My dad was tall, handsome, smart, funny, and driven. He raised his children to live in a world that did not value them. He made us understand that world. He taught us to dream BIG DREAMS. He taught us to really go after those dreams, almost to the exclusion of family, relationships, and self.

There was a single-mindedness about his advice. Don't pursue this option. Do pursue these options.

"Charisse, if you really want to be a teacher, teach Math. Learn about money. Learn about business. Learn about politics. Don't you know the cheese on your sandwich is about math, business, and politics?"

"Daddy," I would say, "I don't like math. I like social studies. How can cheese be political?"

"Charisse, if you want to take care of yourself and your family, learn something that will feed you," he would say.

Dad was quick to point out what he called friends who were imposters. "Charisse, they are not your friends. I see things you don't."

"They are my friends," I would protest. "We go to school together. We sit at the same lunchroom table."

"Charisse, they are not your friends. Listen to me. Clayton is your friend. Carla is your friend. Crystal is your friend. Carlos is your friend. Cathy is your friend. Sheila is your friend. *Your brothers and sisters are your friends. Remember that everything else is a humbug.*"

He was determined that all of us would *be somebody* whatever that meant.

"Charisse," my dad would say, "Listen to Jesse. You are somebody. Now say it, 'I am somebody!' Say it!"

I thought to myself, *Oh my God! When will he stop?* But he didn't stop. He was relentless and he remained relentless during and after his separation and divorce from my mom.

When that time came, I was angry that the "best daddy in the whole wide world" was not coming home anymore. I was angry at him because although my mom was the one who left and kept us with her, I blamed him. I blamed him for not living with us. And no matter what he did, no matter how many times he said, "Your Mama and I could not make it," I blamed him.

Through middle school and several years of high school, I was angry. I was hurt. I was mad. He tried in every way possible to demonstrate in word and deed he was still my dad, and he loved me and my siblings. It did not seem to matter to him that I stopped talking to him. It did not seem to matter that when he came to pick us up that I did not want to go.

When he called, I did not want to talk to him on the phone. I wanted my dad back.

Although I held the phone away from my ear, I could hear him say, "Charisse, are you there? How was school today? What did you learn?"

"Fine," I said. "Nothing," I said. I was not having a conversation with him.

"Charisse, I'm coming to school next week," he told me.

"Okay," I said, and I passed the telephone to one of my sisters quickly.

I did not respond to my dad's letters. It did not matter when he came to the school to talk with my teachers, I did not want him there.

He was relentless about being my dad. It is a relentlessness I now value. It is a relentlessness I treasure. It is a relentlessness I now understand.

Even though I gave up hope for a long season after he left, he never gave up hoping for the possibility we could reconnect. He never gave up on me.

Oddly enough it was my mama who gave me back my dad. She made it clear to me that although she no longer wanted a husband, he was still my dad. And I could love him and want him to be my dad. Mom was direct, "Charisse, I do not need or want for you to hate your dad. He's your dad." She said to me, "Child stay out of grown folks' business!" Mom made it clear it was my choice to love and accept my dad.

Finding my way back to him took time. It took work. It took accepting that he could be my dad, be his own person, and have his own dreams. It took waving at him in the school hallway when he made a visit to see my teacher about my grade (probably a math grade).

It took lingering on the phone half a second longer. It took talking to him. "Daddy, what exactly is a *humbug*? What's *game*?"

"Aww, Charisse, you know a *humbug* when you see one! You know what *game* is? Come on…" I am grateful to my dad for knowing what a little girl and a young woman could not have known at the time: my dad wanted to show up. He wanted to be there for me. He wanted to be my dad. I am grateful for his determination for me to dream big dreams even though I did not know how or why such dreaming was necessary. I am grateful he challenged me to turn my anger into fuel with the question, "To what end Charisse? To what end?" I did not have the perfect dad. (He was never that.) But I did have *the best daddy in the world*.

Grief takes a lot of forms, and it doesn't just come around when someone dies. Absence is a kind of grief that hurts so much. Although we experienced brokenness in our relationship, my dad never accepted brokenness as the final word. He kept reaching out relentlessly, trying to mend the brokenness. He kept showing up with love for me.

Reflection

And I will be a parent to you, and you shall be sons and daughters to me, says the Lord Almighty.

— 2 CORINTHIANS 6:18

My dad did not surrender his role as dad. He was a dad. He showed up when I did not want him to show up. He gave advice when I did not want advice. He was a dad. My prayer for moms and dads is to find ways to interrupt cycles of brokenness and keep reaching out with hope and love.

Charisse, Carlos, Clayton, Crystal, Carla & Cathy Chicago, IL

Sheila, The New Baby

9

SIBLING LOVE

"A sibling is the lens through which you see your childhood."

— ANN HOOD, *DO NOT GO GENTLE* (2014)

A day of celebration

My husband was called to be the Senior Pastor of a Disciples of Christ Church in Lexington, Kentucky, in July 1999. He accepted the call to pastor the church. Fifteen years, four children, and one granddaughter later on a beautiful Saturday morning in July 2014, we were preparing to celebrate his fifteenth pastoral anniversary (mine too as First Lady). The anniversary committee had been planning this celebration for a year. The celebration included hosting a visiting church, a burger build experience, a First Lady Tea, a gala banquet at a fancy dancy hotel, acknowledgments from the General Minister and President of the Christian Church (Disciples of Christ), and a proclamation from the city's mayor. Serving the same church for 15 years was an accomplishment. Growing and healing that same church after years of internal divisions was a big accomplishment. Remaining a loving caring person during such a ministry was quite an accomplishment. We were all ready to share in his well-earned celebration.

And on the day of the big banquet where such recognition was to be given, I got word that my brother had died. The call from my aunt was emotional and painful. But the call started the way most calls from my aunt did with a complaint about me not answering the phone. She said, "You all make me sick. You girls never answer your phones. I know your mom is with your sister in Texas, and she won't pick up the phone. Shit, I'm never calling her again. I called Chicago and they won't answer the phone either."

I listened and then said, "Hi, Aunty. I picked up my phone. What's up?"

She kept going. "Sure, you did Sherry Lynn (her name for me), but you don't usually. Sherry, your brother is dead. I saw the body. He's dead. You are going to have to tell your parents." I knew immediately she meant my younger brother. He was the only one with plans to visit her this weekend.

He is dead

He's dead. I will tell Mom and Dad. All I could think of is: *Why does this shit have to be so hard?* But what I said aloud was, "Okay. He's dead. I'll start making calls."

As I started making calls my husband walked into the room. I said, "Carlos is dead." Over and over again for the next hour that was all I said. *Carlos is dead.* I told my sisters and brother in separate phone calls. They listened but did not say much. I knew they were thinking what I was thinking. Not again. We had lost Cathy ten years ago, and now another one of us has been taken from the circle of love. I made my calls. I waited to get calls, and I sat down on the floor in my bedroom.

I thought about the next few hours. I thought about smiling my way through a banquet. It was too much. I cried. I sobbed. I slept. In a fog, I heard my husband say to the kids. "Leave Mama alone. She's resting."

He tried. But the little people kept coming one by one into our room because they knew that something had disrupted our normal Saturday morning routine. They knew all about the Saturday morning that usually had their names on it was suddenly different – and different not in a good way. Something wasn't right. Finally, he couldn't hold them off any longer and I had to come out of the bedroom. They took one look at my face and said, "What's wrong? Why are you crying?"

I lied. I told them I hurt something and that it made me cry, but it would be okay.

I did not say, "Uncle Carlos is dead." At least I did not say it to the eight-, nine-, ten- or 11-year-olds. I did say it to my 27-year-old who had talked to Carlos just three hours before he died. I did say to him, "Your uncle is dead."

Oddly enough no one asked me, "How did he die?" It was as if we were afraid to ask. Afraid of what we might hear. It was as if we understood there were only a few likely options given his history. A history many of us were praying and praying, and praying some more, was really his history. We were praying the signs of maturity that laced his conversations and behaviors over the past 18 months were strong enough to keep him safe, balanced, and whole. I had hoped his accomplishment as a certified truck driver would reconnect him with the man that he was. I had hoped the confidence placed in him by his employer would be a balm for years of on-again, off-again employment. Not everyone can drive an 18-wheeler successfully. But Carlos could, and he did. I hoped that the welcome of yet another member of his family would tell him, we have not given up on you.

And, then on that day of all days a day of planned celebration for 15 years of faithful ministry, I had to keep saying repeatedly to family. "Yes, it is true. He's dead." In a daze I ate the banquet food, and I lifted my glass in celebration. I took pictures and smiled my way through the anniversary banquet. It was fun.

I arrived at church planning to smile my way through the service, but I was greeted by Elder Channels, Elder Boggs, and Deacon Nuttle. Standing in the church kitchen with our bodies turned towards one another, we created a small circle of privacy. In this temporary bubble, I received words of support and comfort from the Elders and Deacon. Elder Channels, said, "Sister Gillett, Pastor Gillett told me what happened. I just want you to know we are praying for you. Is there something we can do for you? We are praying for you."

In our bubble I whispered, "Elder, I just don't know why this must be so hard all the time. I mean don't we deserve some peace; some joy? I mean really. This feels like a bad movie plot. I find out my brother is dead literally as I am getting dressed for a party celebrating our fifteenth pastoral anniversary. How does that happen? I just don't get it."

"I wish I knew the *why* of many things, but I do not," said Elder Channels. "What I can tell you is that as hard as this is you will be okay someday. Just not today." She hugged me as I tried to hold it together and answer the question she had asked a few minutes ago.

"No, Elder right now, I can't think of anything better you

could do for me but pray. Today is a faith day. There is nothing to do today but hang onto faith."

A circle of sibling love

I know love because of my siblings. These six people love me, and I love them. As kids we did everything together: eat, sleep, fight, argue, play, sneak out of the house, cut the grass, shovel the snow, and even "run away from home together." All of it. I figured out my place in the world in relationship to their place in the world. I understood my gifts and talents as measured against their gifts and talents. I understood my sense of humor as measured against their humor. I measured my hopes and dreams against their ambitions. We fought. We argued. We called each other names. All the same we liked each other. We liked to spend time together. We liked to talk to each other. We loved to read. So, we spent hours at the neighborhood library selecting books for the week. We loved talking to each other and stayed up many nights doing so. We had lofty ideas, and the kitchen table became the place for conversations about those ideas and everything else. The basement became a game room where we talked, played Monopoly, Sorry, Life, and Spades. They were, as my dad said, my friends.

We roamed our south side neighborhood and the city of Chicago. We loved taking the train downtown to State Street. In late November, downtown Chicago was magical with shop owners passing out treats to celebrate the Christmas holiday season. The store windows were decorated in themes from Tchaikovsky's *Nutcracker* or Dickens's *A Christmas Carol*. It was magical. It was a grand adventure ending with a 45-minute wait in line at the Garrett Popcorn shop for a bag of cheese and caramel popcorn mix.

Today I think about the adults we became and the careers

we chose (CPA, Certified Food Health Inspector, economist, educator, union electrician, Certified Truck Driver, city health administrator, and security specialist). I wonder if any of them were as afraid of the future as I felt. I don't know. I do know that because my brother Clayton and sister Carla announced plans to go to college in their final year of high school, all the talk in our house about doing better than our parents and going to college was more than talk. I knew that regardless of what I was thinking, my parents were expecting me to go to college because Clayton and Carla had done so.

They talked openly about college. My brother talked about how much fun it was, and my sister about how to balance her work schedule and class. My brother talked about staying on campus and my sister about going to school at night instead of during the day. They both seemed to look at me and say: *take care of your business*. I knew this because they were following the path my parents had talked about for years, and now they talked openly about college life. They assumed somehow, I was supposed to get into a college. I knew because of them that I HAD to do something so that Crystal, Carlos, Cathy, and Sheila would know that they HAD to do something, too. The words, "each generation must do better than the last generation" echoed in my head. We have to do better than Granny and Granddaddy; we have to do better than Granma Rose. We must do better than Mama and Daddy. We have to go to college. We must advance the game. We have to do better. We must do better. It was a mantra.

Decades later after many college graduations, several professional accomplishments, and dozens of hard conversations around the table, we had to reckon with the death of Cathy before her thirtieth birthday and Carlos in his early fifties. In these most difficult moments, my siblings gave me strength. They gave me courage. It was our collective memories of each other that gave me strength and that I called upon when Cathy and Carlos became angels. On both occasions, I remember asking God, "Why does this have to be so hard?" I remember sobbing and hanging onto my own hard-won faith. And to the love and memories of my siblings.

Reflection

I will sing of your steadfast love, O Lord, forever; with my mouth I will proclaim your faithfulness to all generations.

— PSALM 89:1

My prayer for siblings is that you remember the ties that bind you together in love, challenge, and joy. I pray that you remember and celebrate that you are the results of generations of hope, and it is in pursuit of that generational hope that I embrace evidence of God's faithfulness and mercy to me and you. It is impossible to be who we are today without giving thanks to the generations of saints who prayed us into this century. God is faithful generation after generation after generation and for the generations to come.

Mom and Dad

Don and Me, 60th Birthday Celebration Lexington, KY
January 16, 2022

CALL THE ROLL

O nce a year the congregation comes together for the annual congregational meeting. The preparation for this meeting starts in late August or early September with a review of budget requests for outstanding mission work, a review of ministry reports, and reports from the pastoral relations and property committees. Preparation for the annual meeting also includes multiple discussions about what it means to be on the church roll. Being on the church roll at the congregational meeting means one can vote on matters of importance. It means that one is invested in the issues of importance to the community of faith. It means that one has given of their time, testimony, treasure, and tithe. It means that one shows up for the people and congregation as an expression of one's personal faith and commitment to the whole church. People want to be on the church roll. They want to be counted. On the day of the annual congregational meeting, the gathering always includes people one does not recognize, others one would see frequently but not every Sunday, and those who are the hands and feet and heart and soul of the congregation. They are all there waiting for the start of the annual church meeting.

This particular year, the chair of the board is wearing a black suit and black hat decorated with flowers and a green pin. She sits on the left side of the church on the first pew to ensure quick access to the floor microphone. The pastor is wearing a black robe with an Advent stole with the words hope, joy, peace, and love draped around his shoulders. He waits behind the pulpit. Following a prayer by the deacon of the month, the elder stands, nods to the chair of the board and then the pastor. Then he turns to face the congregation. In a loud voice he says, "Good afternoon church. I call the roll."

I witnessed this Roll Call year after year, and it has become for me a metaphor of support in my own life. Each year I try to remember those friends, family, teachers, and coaches who over the years have been a source of wisdom, knowledge, and support to me.

It's hard to know who I would have become without others who invested in me and showed up with their time, testimony, treasure, and faith in my life. By the time that little girl who was me had graduated from high school and left for college, I had found a way to reach out to others with my doubts and to talk about my fears. I was teaching myself how to protect my mind and spirit from my harmful thoughts. I was teaching myself to ignore the self-doubt that led me to say out loud, *I want to kill myself.*

I told myself to ignore the counselor at my high school that said, "You are not college material because of your test scores." I ignored the teacher who said, "You are not smart enough to take honors history because of your test scores." I tried hard to dismiss the teacher who said, "Because of your test scores you'll drop out of college after one semester."

I was learning how to disentangle myself from covertly competitive and unhealthy relationships. With some of my friends it was always something. It was always nothing, but it wasn't good. Too many sly comments. Too many times I would hear, "Girl, we're just playing" after hurtful comments. Too many times I headed home almost in tears after hanging out with them. I could hear my dad saying these relationships were a *humbug*. I finally understood he was right, and they were hurting me.

I tried hard to dismiss adult voices that confirmed my fears that I was not smart enough for the next level. Because *that little girl* was my priest, because I had prayer warriors around me, because I sought support and received support, because I heard my mother saying, "It will be alright," I was learning to listen and trust the good within me. I was trying hard to discern the hopeful possibilities within me. Most of all I was learning to draw upon the love of my family and trust their encouragement to push me past the fear, self-doubt, hurt, and disappointments I felt, both real and imagined. Ultimately, their voices of support and encouragement, my desire not to disappoint them, and an embryonic faith made me venture into the world.

I was learning to listen to and for God's voice from every direction.

By the time I reached college, I was both fragile *and* strong. I was scared *and* determined. I was both aware of the gift of my life *and* aware of how close I came to not having life at all. I arrived at college aware of my responsibility to live, not to disappoint my family, and to graduate. I knew my older sister wanted to go away, but she stayed home and worked while attending college. She sent me $10.00 a month to use for fun money. Her hard-earned gift reminded me I could not drop out and come home without a degree. EVERYONE in my family circle believed in me. They thought I could do it.

It was difficult shutting out the voices that told me *I could not achieve* and voices that reminded me *what I could not do* and voices that reminded me *what I had not done*. Giving attention to the good voices took practice. Giving attention to the voices that encouraged my aspirations and encouraged my unformed dreams and hopes took practice. I learned to trust those who had trusted me with the high school newspaper, the Prom Committee, and the French Club. I learned to accept the help that I needed to understand algebra and biology. I learned to ignore those who would forecast my destiny based upon my zip code, test scores, race, and gender. They missed the evidence I put in front of their eyes. I learned to listen for the voices that saw my promise even when I could not see it myself. I guess I learned to be hopeful. I learned to harness my fears, frustrations, and doubts. I learned to accept the encouragement of living breathing examples of Black love, female strength, and kindness.

To honor them and their importance in the life of *that little girl*... me, I wear a black robe with three light blue bars. I stand as a seminary president, mother, wife, and friend, and I call the roll.

I call the roll of the women, young girls, teachers from my childhood and youth who called that little girl in me into courage and life: Vivian Brown, Linda Boayue , Eugenia Brown, Rose Floyd, Lilly Irene Brown, Armetta Gathings, Agnes Jones, Lillian Davis, Caroline Bonds, Linda, Marva, Billy Ann, Carol Jean, Janis, Juniata Wright, Ms. Clarice, Ms. Callie, Ms. McAlister, Ms. McGhee, Ms. Saulsberry, Grizelda, Carla, Crystal, Cathy, Sheila B., Sheila S., Janita Faye, Marigold, Sherry, Tanya, Lisa, Stephanie, Rhonda, Brenda, Ruth Anderson, Chrissy Frye, Ms. Jacaric, Ms. Bigenia, Ms. Novak, Ms. Stienne, and Ms. Mattie.

I call the roll of the men who helped me recognize the goodness of manhood: Clayton G. Brown, Stephen Brown, Crusmon Brown, Oliver Davis Sr., Mr. Macalister, Clifford

Bonds Sr., Clayton L, Carlos, Monty, Micheal, Eddie, LaMarr, Jamal, and Lacy.

I call the roll for my cousins, family, friends and colleagues from across the life of the church and in higher education. All of you uniquely encouraged my voice and imagination to claim my life, my dreams, and my hopes for my life.

I call the roll for the women and in particular Black women who modeled leadership for me. You did not know me, but I saw you. I heard you. I celebrate you for showing me that Black Girl dreams could be real.

DR. CHARISSE L. GILLETT

Reflection

In all things, offering yourself as a model of good works and in your teaching offering integrity, gravity, and sound speech that cannot be censured.

— TITUS 2:7-8A

My hope for you is that you can also rise and call the roll of those who have loved you into being fully *you*. I invite you to give thanks for those who held you together, for those who shared wisdom and gave your insight, and for those who poured into you when you could not pour into yourself. I pray you pass on the blessing by showing up for those who need you.

Me, Summer 2024, Versailles, KY

EPILOGUE

THE REST OF THE STORY

The scared young woman who took the bus to Iowa City was not sure what was next. Yet she was determined to succeed, and for many she is an example of success. However, that is the rest of the story.

The rest of the story is one of a young woman who learned to navigate spaces that professor and author Melissa Harris Perry calls *crooked rooms*. She learned to navigate spaces that did not welcome her or believe in her. Spaces that often made her presence a referendum on one or more social, political, and/or cultural agendas. In such spaces she learned to adapt. On more than one occasion she contorted her physical, social, emotional, and spiritual self to fit into spaces designed for others, spaces unwilling to yield or make room for her. On more than one occasion she completely lost her composure, held her tongue to keep her job and plotted a comeback.

The rest of the story is that of a young woman who through trial, error, tears, anger, and a shallow and deep faith persisted and kept going. A special thanks to those who offered support and counsel in crooked rooms and pulpits and for opening doors that gave me the opportunity to be my best self. Because of their support and that of many others, that little girl learned how to enter rooms and shift energy so that she could offer her most authentic self to the ministry to which God called her.

www.ingramcontent.com/pod-product-compliance
Lightning Source LLC
Chambersburg PA
CBHW061707120626
46550CB00003B/1122